Amritanjali

Swami Turiyamritananda Puri

Mata Amritanandamayi Center, San Ramon
California, United States

Amritanjali, by Swami Turiyamritananda Puri.
Translated from the original Malayalam by Prof. V. Muraleedhara Menon.

Published by:
  Mata Amritanandamayi Center
  P.O. Box 613
  San Ramon, CA 94583
  United States

Copyright © 1996 by Mata Amritanandamayi Mission Trust, Amritapuri, Kerala 690546, India

No portion of this book, except for brief review, may be reproduced, stored in a retrieval system, or transmitted in any form or by any means—electronic, mechanical, photocopying, recording, or otherwise—without written permission of the publisher.

First edition by the MA Center: October 2016

Address in India:
  Mata Amritanandamayi Mission Trust
  Amritapuri, Kollam Dt.
  Kerala 690546, India
  www.amritapuri.org
  inform@amritapuri.org

Mother, all my songs are but the lispings of Your ignorant child ever clutching at You as my only refuge in this dreadful samsara of endless shadows. I offer them at Your Holy Feet in wordless love.

—Swami Turiyamritananda

A Word in Gratitude

A blessed soul who had the fortune to drink in Amma's nectarine affection to his heart's content, gifted with an uncommon felicity of expression, marked by a rich sense of humour, a luminous intellect, above all, a tender and loving heart—all these qualities portray the personality of Shri Muraleedhara Menon, who has rendered these poems into English from the original Malayalam.

A gifted orator and writer, he has enriched our mother tongue by translating many valuable works of Swami Ranganathananda from English into Malayalam. Though I have a longstanding intimate friendship with him, I am moved to express my profound gratitude to him, for having undertaken this task of his own initiative, moved solely by a heart brimming with love and devotion to Amma.

Two other names worthy of remembrance in this context are—Sister Varenya who did the layout and typesetting, and Brother Arun who took much pain to bring this book to light.

—Swami Turiyamritananda Puri

Foreword

A stern God, remote from us and the world, terror-striking, not love-inspiring, is revolting to our sensibility. Divinity is the essence of our consciousness, infilling everything, pervading everywhere, impelling all, revealing Itself as Pure Being, Bliss and Wisdom. This is not just a pet creed or idea, but the direct experience of countless seekers down the ages who have felt the stirring of the Spirit within to break open the little prison of their organic individuality and lose themselves in the Divine. It is Light, Sweetness, Freedom and Fulfilment. India has produced a succession of saints who have sung and danced their way to God, sweetening and sanctifying the earth. Sometimes Divinity itself incarnates in a human body to save people from hideous materialism which is plain sensualism. The impact an Incarnation produces is profound and pervasive, liberating the earnest, guiding the groping, lifting the fallen and comforting the afflicted, thus

leavening the earth. In our times, Amma's advent has a global significance.

Here is a bunch of poems and songs by Swami Turiyamritananda Puri. Lacking formal education and with nothing to call his own in the material world, he was guided by destiny to Amma and has been Her protege since then. The budding Poet in him has been flowering in Amma's inspiring presence. His life is ever centred on Amma, who is his unfailing inspiration, the melody, theme and tune of all his songs.

The reader will notice in these poems different moods —the very groping and seeking, the sheer joy of finding final refuge at the feet of his Guru and God, the pangs of separation, and the calm assurance of the ultimate merger into the Great Being—so characteristic of all earnest sadhaks.

It is difficult to capture in translation the spirit of the original.

My pranams to Amma.

Prof. V. Muraleedhara Menon

Contents

Foreword — 5

Prose — 9
Refuge — 10
The Mad, Divine Love — 17

Poems — 29
She is Our Amma — 31
The Soul's Mantra — 33
The Wish-Fulfilling Tree — 36
Nothing is Ours — 39
The Pranava Mantra Incarnate — 42
With Love — 44
Cure for the Existential Anguish — 46
The River of Life — 49
At Your Feet — 51
Dew Drop — 55
The Tree of Knowledge — 58
Before Creation — 60
You are Far, Yet Near — 62

The Holy Confluence	64
Will My Krishna Ever Come?	66
Mother of All	68
The Treasure of Experience	70
My Heart, A Temple	73
Hymn to Ganga	76
Let my Heart Be a Flower at Your Feet	78
May You Fare Well	80
Rain Cloud	82
My Heart, A Flower at Her Altar	84
Peace at Last	85
Dedication	87
Salutation	91
The New Dawn	92
Glossary of Sanskrit Terms	96

Prose

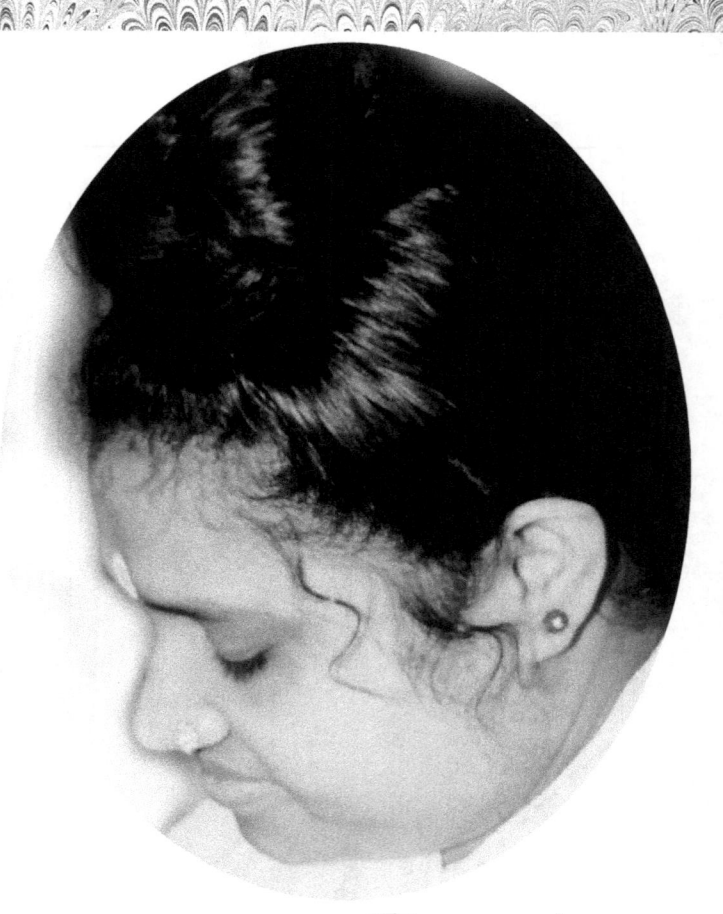

Refuge

I stood before that Divine Splendour, transfixed. My heart, bathed in bliss, lay prostrate at those Holy Feet which break all bonds and shatter all samsaric illusion.

In those stormy days of my vague, weary search which led me nowhere, I would become desperate sometimes and cry out, "Discard me, Lord, let me perish." Sometimes I would meekly say, "Lead me as You will."

I wandered on and on, trekking long distances. Poor me, clutching at my own hand I was circling round myself!

The way that lay before me was too long and windy for my sore feet to cover.

I had no thought of where I should reach to end my uncertain wandering. After all, there was no destination for me to arrive at.

I had no belongings, no money; I was relieved of all such useless burdens. I had long been inured to hunger and thirst. I ate gluttonously the remnants of cooked rice which the untouchables would somehow scrape up and offer in their earthen bowl with the touch of love. The upper class forbade me lest I should be polluted, but I had outgrown all such taboos.

I would sit idly on the bank of the canal and watch with unconcern the last boat leaving the jetty. I would pick, now and then, the prickly leaves of the sprawling grass and throw them, one by one, into the wavy water. I was joyed

to see them whirling round and round in the eddies. I too was, in a way, whirling in the endless eddies of uncertainties. I would move on aimlessly in the inky darkness of the silent night. My feet were leaving behind long tracks. Was it that, unawares, I was moving slowly, haltingly, towards the sanctuary of my soul?

None showed me the way that leads to the throne of God. Angels I found not on the way.

Stars were blinking drowsily. Old shrivelled trees on the wayside were asleep. The bitter cold was piercing my bones. Yet I did not rest or sleep. I was inching my way through blinding darkness. Where or why I did not know. Some power was spurring me on.

Ah! The frightful loneliness was an unnerving experience, but slowly I became used to it. Now solitude is my delightful companion.

I came across various people, all strangers, and they went as they came. In fact, I was a stranger to myself. What the sensitive modern writers call self-alienation is the most torturing experience of the soul, and I have had enough of it. Those who have felt it alone know its awful agony.

Now when I look back, my long sessions with my alien self with all its anguish, disgust and rage leap into my memory with a pleasant sensation.

Why didn't I cry then?

To tell the truth, I was afraid of even crying.

Seasons changed in rhythmic succession. Plantation work in the paddy fields had begun. Fresh water was being pumped in to flood the parched fields. The pale shreds of clouds which had emptied their burdens of water were strewn here and there on the blue sky. The paddy seedlings, tender and green, were swaying and dancing gleefully in knee-deep water. My mind alone lay like a wasteland, starved, dry and desolate.

Onam came, the unique festival of the land. People, young and old, were all agog for this great event. The immortal Mahabali, the mythical king, is said to emerge from the underworld to visit his land and his people once in a year. All the tragedies, privations, miseries and cares of the yesteryear melt into the heady joy of the Onam festival. What would this great king think of me if perchance he would meet me on the way, I thought. I must be an evil omen to his eyes, I feared.

Time slipped by. A lone wanderer in a strange world, I had nothing to clutch at as my own. In me was a volcano erupting, a storm raging. The world and its people had ceased to exist for me long ago. I was groping for an anchorage for the frail vessel of my life cast adrift on the rough waters of death and destruction. I was panting and pining for my heart's Beloved. Sometimes I would lapse into a mood of hopeless despair and give myself up as lost, but it would not last long. When failure and frustration stared me in the face, something within seemed to whisper, "Go on, don't lose heart". Hope kindled, I would continue my lonely trek. Again darkness, fear and pessimism. But now the inner voice was clear, "Seek and you shall find." I was elated with joy and told myself that my hungry eyes would feast on the vision of my Beloved, which would wipe off forever the pangs, fears and anxieties of my storm-tossed soul and instill into it lasting bliss and peace.

Looking back, I find to my delight that this still small voice which I heard within came true. I found at last my Guru, my Mother, my All-in-all. Then I sang in spontaneous joy:

> "The wick of the lamp in the yonder temple
> Keeps burning steadily
> To beckon the wayfarer groping in the dark."

Again I sang:
  "My Mother is the rare celestial tree
  That ever shades and shelters,
  Sates and fills every weary soul."

Again:
  "My Mother of immortal bliss pours in profusion
  Love nectarine into the heart that unfolds."

I stood before that Divine Splendour, transfixed. My heart, bathed in bliss, lay prostrate at those Holy Feet which break all bonds and shatter all samsaric illusion. What I felt and experienced is too sacred to be profaned by words; let that holy memory be my unshared possession in my earthly sojourn.

But, then, this Truth flashed that my real search had only begun. Again, the search? Yes, but the search now is straight like an arrow darted from the bow, sure to hit the target. The Path before me is lit up, my Mother grips my hand; the goal, though distant, is clearly sighted and I am assured of reaching it. Ah! What more to ask for! My only prayer is:

  "Accept me, Mother, out of Your boundless
  compassion. Poor me, I have nothing to offer but this

frail, unscented flower of my heart; sanctify it with Your touch, make it worthy of being placed at Your feet as my final worship."

The Mad, Divine Love

She was love and courage personified. I should say that Her love was aggressive. She conquered all with that. Only the Divine can love those who hate, bless those who vilify.

Those were terrible days, in a way, blessed days! What an agonising search! I was moving about in a strange world like an alien and was home-sick. Even though I could not spell it out then, it was a spiritual hunger which kept me on the move, restless and tortured. I was just a boy, innocent of the world and its ways. I wandered at large. It seemed I was floating down a rushing stream in spite of myself and I was struggling hard to get ashore. Sometimes I felt I was lost, sometimes dark fears would oppress me.

Yet I was struggling—a life and death struggle. My uncertain wanderings, my frantic search led me nowhere. I was desperate.

One day, in the course of my wandering, I reached the small Vallickavu village and there I saw the Holy Mother. She was very young then and was passing through extraordinary spiritual states. I could not understand those states then. But something gripped me, stirred me, the very sight of Her was soothing, pacifying. But I was not sure whether She could give me spiritual refuge.

My previous experiences of many Gurus had made me wary. Moreover, it was difficult to visit Her often in those days because Her family would curtly turn away any outsider. No doubt, the Mother had fascinated me; but I was in no mood for acceptance. My urge was to go to the Himalayas which seemed to beckon me. Being inexperienced and penniless, I had limitations. Physical hardships which were many did not daunt me. But in my mind there was the fierce battle between the primal instincts and higher aspirations. I was torn between two worlds, but my spirit could never compromise with the world of the senses. I was undergoing a fiery ordeal, what the mystics call 'the darkness of the Soul'! I did not relent my struggle, my search. One more year slipped by and I was all the more restless. Who could imagine the storm raging in my heart then!

I met the Mother again. It was not my choosing but Her willingness that made it possible. I felt a sudden urge to see Her and so I went. My lips were muttering the lines of the cry of my heart:

"Birds that fall with clipped wings have the earth
to hold,
Who will shelter the unsheltered me, Mother?"

Rays of Love

The Mother, holding both my hands, looked into my misty eyes with Her smile, out of Her eyes shot rays of Love and Grace which flooded my whole being. I was bathed in bliss and peace. Every cell of my body was vibrant with a new life. I felt as if I was reborn. Words fail to express even feebly that transforming experience. Full of compassion, the Mother whispered into my ears: "Are you still crying? Believe that you have taken refuge at the Feet of the Divine Mother."

My Mother heard the anguished cry of my heart. Or else, where would I have been now? Left to myself, I would have fallen on the wayside like an autumn leaf blown away by the winds. I would have died in the cocoon of my dark fears and vain imaginings. Ah! I tremble to think of it all now.

I feel blessed because I have found shelter at the Feet of the Divine Mother after a long and aimless spiritual odyssey. Even so, in the initial period, I doubted whether fate would sweep me into the world of Maya. "O, my Love incarnate Mother, am I destined to be deluded by Maya?", I used to ask in a song of mine. I prayed to the Mother, night and day, for saving me from slipping into the world of Maya, and filling me with the mad, all-forgetting spiritual

bliss. Once I asked Her in utter despair, "Mother, I have totally surrendered myself to You, yet why don't You shower Your Grace on me?" But my mind was full of Her, my lips were muttering Her Mantra.

Another day, in a sudden spurt of courage, I asked, "If I am not worthy of Your Grace, who else is worthy, Mother?"

I mention all these things here just to highlight the different phases of the evolution of a sadhaka's mind until he is firmly established in the life of the Spirit. The sadhaka's mind will persist in rebelling, revolting, testing, questioning and doubting until it is purged of all its old impressions inherited from countless past lives, cleansed and made a fit receptacle for the Divine Grace. Today those memories are my priceless treasures.

A Challenge

Spiritual life is a challenge. I was battling against my lower nature as well as the external forces. There was the problem of physical existence to boot. In that most trying period, I was sustained by my Mother spiritually and emotionally. She was the centre of my life.

Mother was bafflingly strange and mysterious in Her moods. None could gauge Her depth. She concealed Her real personality behind a thick veil of feigned ignorance and indifference. I had a little innate spiritual sensitivity, so I could instinctively feel that with all Her pretence to the contrary, She had a profound spiritual depth. She could not 'deceive' me. I had occasions later to catch glimpses of the real Mother which She revealed in some unguarded moments.

She was love and courage personified. The ignorant society incapable of understanding Her high spiritual states, ecstasies and trances, Her utter unconventionality and queer behaviour, opposed, criticised and maligned Her wildly. The Mother stood them all with Her cherubic smile. She was all love even to Her worst detractors. Critics, opponents and devotees were alike to Her; Her motherly heart enfolded all of them. I should say that Her love was aggressive. She conquered all with that. Only the Divine can love those who hate, bless those who vilify.

Now the situation has changed. The very critics have been compelled to admit Her greatness. People throng to Her in large numbers from far and near, even from abroad for spiritual enlightenment, for peace, for the lessening of life's

burdens, for finding meaning and stability in their fragile and frivolous lives.

Constant Miracle

The greatest miracle of the Mother is the Power of Her Love which is creative and transforming. I have seen with my own eyes how She transforms hatred into love, poison into nectar. This is Her constant miracle. What greater miracle is there than the infusion of the nectarine love into the parched hearts, night and day, without caring for Her body and its minimum needs.

People mostly are fascinated by miracles and so they are eager to hear the miracles Mother performs. I for one have never seen any such. She is absolutely natural and simple in all Her dealings with the people. Her spontaneous Love is Her miracle. She is the Mother to all who come to Her, irrespective of their merits or demerits. She guides them, protects them and unfolds their personality into the light of the spirit. Love is Her speech and service is Her action. I should like to say firmly that the readiness to serve all with the spirit of sacrifice which the Mother exemplifies in Her life is the only miracle we should strive to attain. A life rich in active love is the only power we should care to

possess. This profound lesson we have learnt at the feet of our Mother.

Many have visited the Mother to test Her and they have been tested in turn, but none has been sent away empty-handed; She has quickened their spirit without their knowing. Those who have sought shelter have found shelter at Her Holy Feet. The genuine struggling souls who have rushed to Her for liberation have been vouchsafed that boon.

We need not despair for the worldly and the unspiritual who refuse to let in the light of the spirit to illumine their dark minds and shrivelled spirit. They cannot swim against the current long. The dynamics of evolution will push them up. Evolution is through time and it is always upward: it is quick in the case of a few, and slow and halting for the majority, but evolve they should.

When the clouds of ignorance, untruths and sins that darken the soul are removed, we experience the glory, immensity and purity of our soul. We develop there an inner eye which sees into the subtle realms of Truth. With that eye alone can we identify a Divine Incarnation.

Universal Motherhood

The Mother once said, "Remember, I will never desert whoever has sought refuge in Me". No saint can give this assurance, only an incarnation can. That explains the constant state of Her universal Motherhood. My concept of divinity is this, so I have laid myself at the feet of the Mother in utter surrender.

In my inward journey through meditation, the Mother has guided me at every step and what I am today is Her making. I am sure that She has accepted my silent self-offering and worship and that She will bestow on me the Grace of life-fulfillment.

Her supreme love has made me a slave and today I have nothing to claim as mine; everything—me and mine—belongs to Her. So I do not bow down before Her anymore. Why should I? My life itself is a salutation to the Mother. Those who criticise me for not indulging in the external acts of showy sentimental piety miss the spirit of true surrender. They are superficial; only their heads have bent low, not their hearts.

God is personal as well as impersonal. A personal God has a heart that melts in compassion to all human afflictions, cries, petitions and prayers. My Divine Mother has that

compassionate heart. So I prayed to Her once, "Mother, I am Your son, and I surrender myself and mine to You; accept me, Mother, accept me. I am innocent, so throw me not into the hands of death, my Mother." She has heard my sobbing prayer and Her assurance buoys me up in all situations. My frail ship has found the haven and I am secure.

That I have been blessed by this Divinity is the Supreme fortune which is possible only through Her Grace. Not the severest austerities of many lives can attain this rarest fortune of living daily with a Divine Incarnation.

I am thrilled with joy and pride that I found my Holy Mother and laid myself at Her Feet years ago in my tender age.

Let me strive hard to make my life meaningful. Let my life be enriched by love, patience and the readiness to serve. Let me plunge into myself deeper and deeper and come face to face with my soul in that transcendental awareness which is the ultimate purpose of human evolution. May I then like a dew drop melt into the ocean of Sat-Chit-Ananda (Absolute Existence, Absolute Consciousness, Absolute Bliss). I pray to the Mother for me and for you all. Won't you pray for me likewise? Mother has taught us this lesson of brotherhood and togetherness in spirit.

From this ocean of nectarine love let us draw as much as our cupped palms can hold, sip a little and distribute the rest among others, which will cleanse and sanctify their hearts. May the Holy Mother bless us all to realise the best in our lives!

Om Peace! Peace! Peace!

Poems

She is Our Amma

Amma is ever a mystery baffling our understanding,
She is all love and tenderness,
Wisdom perfect, sweetness nectarine;
She is Bliss to be experienced, but unknowable;
Still, She is our Amma.

She is the Truth of the universe,
Goodness inherent in all,

The perennial shower of Grace,
Far, yet near;
Still, She is our Amma.

She is Compassion illimitable,
Not a person, but the Supreme Principle
Beyond all dualities,
The very essence of all existence;
Still, She is our Amma.

She is the origin and spirit of the Pranava Mantra,
The rhythm and harmony of the divine melody of the
 Soul,
The unfailing response to our trust and call,
The uncomposed poem, the unsung song;
Still, She is our Amma.

She is the sweetest word ever, other words are empty;
For, She is infinite, perfect, eternally delightful;
She is the Light that lighteth all lights;
Still, She is our Amma.

The Soul's Mantra

Aum Amriteshwaryai Namah.
    The Mantra fills and floods
    heart and soul,
        The Mantra illumines
        the path and the goal
        eternal,
            The Mantra evokes
            the Bliss of the
            Self awakened.

When the Divine Mother, caressing the fevered limbs,
Darts one tender look of melting Compassion,
All the darkness of delusion vanishes in no time,
And the aching mind reposes in the vast peace of
   the Self.

When Amma blesses in Her boundless Grace,
All afflictions past cure cease to be,
All the haunting fears, pains, are gone,
And the samsaric bondage of the Jiva is shattered.

When Amma showers Her wondrous Love,
The drooping spirit is stirred, quickened,
It wakes and is illumined
In the fadeless light of the deathless Soul.

The Wish-Fulfilling Tree

Sweetest Mother, You give away boons Your children ask for,
You bestow soul-bliss on the earnest seekers,
You assure refuge to the weary, vexed and lost,
Come, Mother, abide ever in my heart's small shrine.

Since my memories woke up and my Spirit was stirring,
The timid poet in me has been shaping my heart's
 melodies to Your tune,
I have been seeking You through my songs,
 day and night,
Forgetting me and the world around like one possessed.

I have been a lone pilgrim, groping, stumbling, yet
 trekking,
Dead-set to drop this frail flower at Your Lotus-Feet.
I have stopped at each flower blooming, each cloud
 sailing,
Fancying in my ignorance to see in them Your angelic face
 with its beatific smile.

Now I know all my aching past
And fearsome future were illusion's creations.
I am living in the eternal 'Now',
In my Mother's Timeless Being.

Nothing is Ours

Relations are delusions, they belong to us not,
All that's ours is our own soul, pure, holy and eternal.
This little life will end soon, casting off all its belongings,
The Soul alone is here and hereafter, through eternity.

No one dead carries with him his much-vaunted possessions,
No one living accompanies the dear departed to the world beyond.
Man tarries here in an alien world for a while,
Why, then, this mad scramble for things that leave him soon?

*Know for certain that the Truth of life is the soul within,
It is futile to chase it in the world without;
Delving deep in one daring leap,
We come face to face with our Self immortal.*

*The waves of grief that rock many a ship of life
Are stilled and dare not enter the soul's haven of peace.
The Self reveals itself to the questing, daring,
   heroic ones,
Who have shuttered the ego and the bondage it has
   wrought.*

*To move from the unreal to the Real and ever abide in It
Is life's fulfilment supreme, bliss and peace absolute.*

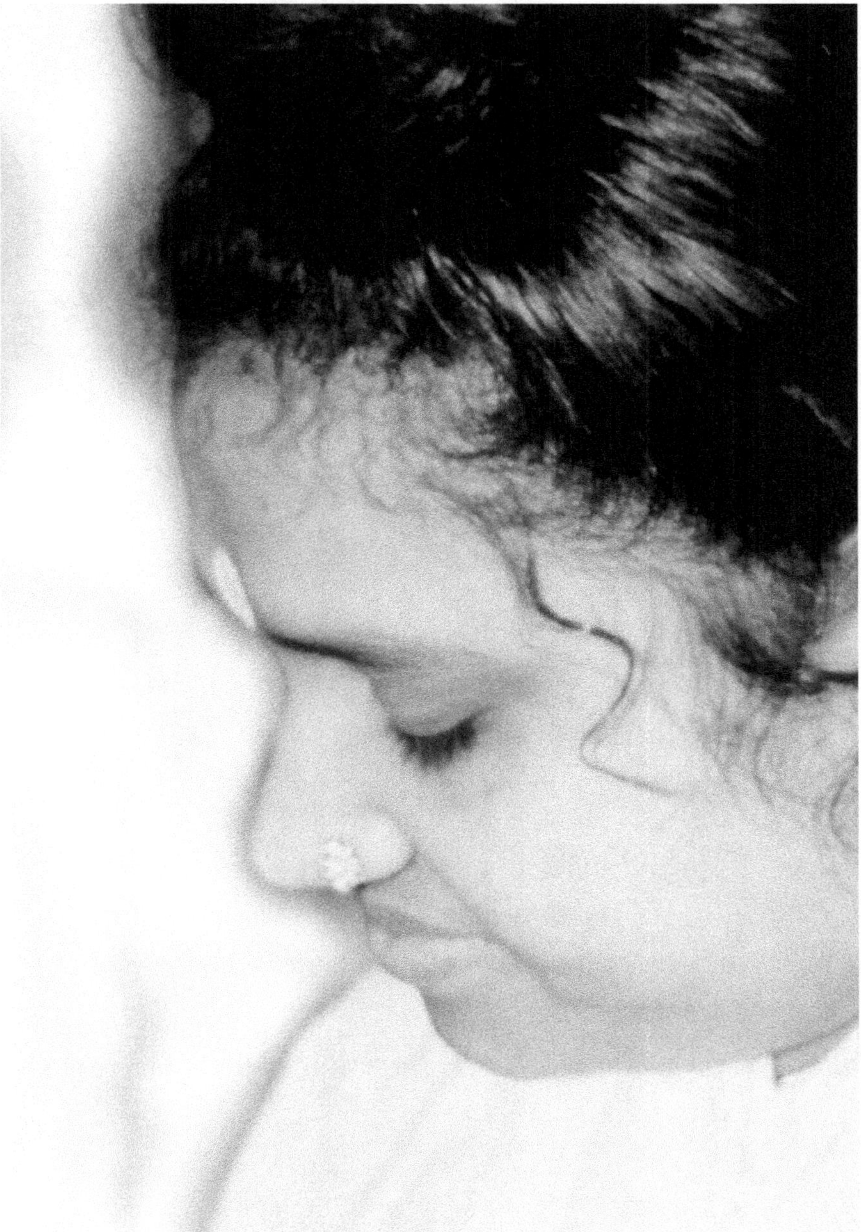

The Pranava Mantra Incarnate

You are the Pranava Mantra Incarnate,
  giving away gifts of genius,
Inspiring the Muses into creations varied, splendid.
I am Your little child trailing along behind You,
Ever pestering You to quicken the timid poet in me.

I pray You, Mother, to keep my heart's spring ever full,
And let it cascade in a limpid flow of ceaseless songs.
What are my songs, Ma, but my sullen heart's silent
  sobs?
Give them the touch of Your Grace, transmute them into
  melodies sweet.

With Love

Accept, Mother, my heart's wordless salutation,
My soul's silent adoration.
You are Truth and Bliss incarnate,
Bestow Your Grace on me, Your poor child.

I have been craving for it,
I have been crying for it,
I am lone, forlorn, languishing,
Quicken my listless spirit with a touch.

The lavish dispenser of countless gifts,
Come, Ma, as the all-purifying Ganga,
As the shower of all-sweetening nectar,
Quench the thirst of my parched soul.

You are the ocean of compassion to the afflicted,
Soul-filling bliss to the weary pilgrims.
My little heart, like a butterfly on the wings of song
Is ever humming around the unfading blossom
of Your Love.

My heart is sore, vexed, darkened
As if stung by a venomous serpent,
I am groping in a blinding night,
Come, Mother, like the fresh dawn of illumination.

Cure for the Existential Anguish

When that Divine face wreathed in beatific smile
Shines in the heart's white expanse,
Then alone will cease all the anguish of earth-chained
   existence.

I am a storm-tossed soul, blinded,
Unsure of the way, groping, weary, vexed.
When will my soul awake in You, my fondest Mother?

You bless all who seek and ask,
You are the proverbial wish-fulfilling tree,
Why not take pity on my crushed, bleeding heart?

Don't You feel, Mother, the pangs of my sullen heart?
I have been adoring You long and am tired now,
Flood my parched heart with a fresh shower
    of all-devouring devotion.

Can my poor little brain ever know Your Divine
    Majesty?
You reveal Yourself to hearts made pure by mad divine
    love,
Streaming forth as nectarine sweetness flooding the whole
    being.

My restless heart is pining for You day and night,
It is athirst for Your ambrosial love.
Slake the thirst, fulfil it, dissolve it in Your Infinite
    Being.

The River of Life

Let the river of life glide along gaily
To join at last the infinite ocean of silence;
To merge into the Ocean of Sat, Chit, Ananda.

The sea-water evaporates massing into swollen clouds,
Which again rain down to become the flowing rivers,
Rushing, hurrying to empty into the ocean.

Our experiences, varied though, have a purpose in the
    Divine Play,
Our life running in windy ways is goaded by an urge
To lose and fulfil itself in the Great Beyond, the Divine.

The river of life thus flows on and on,
Deepening in experience and wisdom;
Let it glide on smoothly, without a hitch,
For the final tryst with its Lord.

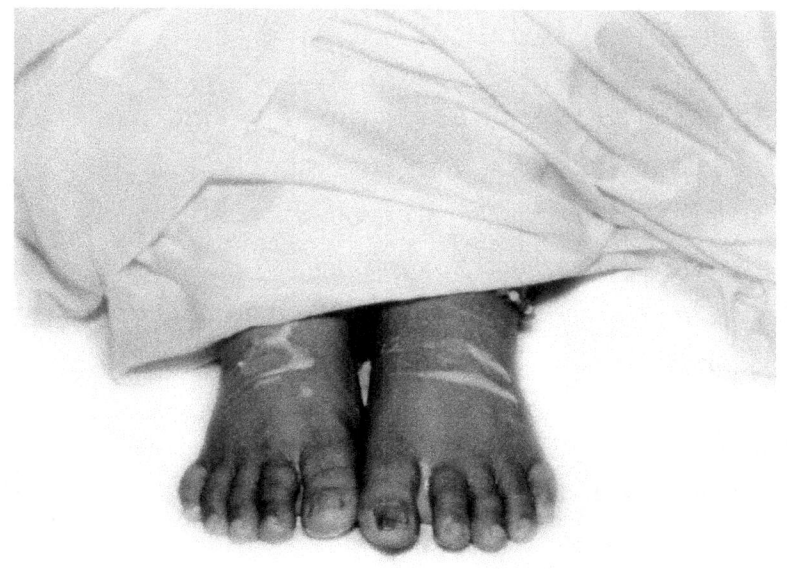

At Your Feet

Mother, You have incarnated umpteen times before,
Riding the Chariot of dharma across the darkened earth;
I have been with You always, a weeny child,
Crying, nagging, vexing, yet ever clinging.

Still I am the same little child, nestling unto You,
Crawling around, lying at Your feet.
Your love soothing, wisdom profound,
    are cascades of bliss flooding my heart;
Your Divine Face with its beatific smile lights up a new
    dawn.

Your love so unearthly, copious, free
Pervades my inner being like the cool moonlight,
And my heart becomes a lamp with thousand flames
Which I wave before You in silent adoration.

When You lift the sagging spirit of Your children
With fondest kisses and tenderest love,
And shower endless compassion on one and all,
The world, it seems, stands transfixed in thrill.

Dew Drop

I am a dew drop at the far edge of a tiny leaf of
   grass,
Alive awhile, aching, tremulous, delicately poised,
Dripping, emptying, and will be no more.

Poor me, can I ever scan the mystery of the mazy world,
Time's ceaseless motion, its drift, thrust and goal?
Cramped in the world, bound in time, can I ever know
    the transcendental Truth?

Crazy and deluded, I take for real
What light and shade shape——fleeting chimeras;
What their endless play conjures up——frothy nothings.

Light casts shadows, they cease when light is no more;
Ah! the myriad forms, all lovely, spring into sight in
    light;
But where are they when the light illumines them not?

I gaze and gaze at the blooming flower, scented and
    flushed,
I am enchanted by its swaying and smiling,
And give it rapturous praise in my thoughtless ignorance.

But what a fool I make of myself
Not to know that frail beauty will drop ere sun-down,
Not to know that my bursting dreams will die alike.

When the 'immeasurable' time I seek to 'measure'
The 'I' fades away, 'You' and 'all' are all erased;
If 'I' am not, who is to know whom?
    ——A void absolute.

When the 'unfathomable' ocean I seek to fathom,
I dissolve into the vast roaring brine together with
    my rod;
Ah! then, there is no 'me' to swim ashore to tell
    its depth.

The Tree of Knowledge

Mother, You are the primordial Tree of Knowledge,
Unto which fly home the cosmic birds for their nest.
I pray You to shelter me under Your ambient shade
Till You in Your Grace reveal the Truth
    and dissolve me.

The blue sky, so sing the Vedas, is Your crowned Head,
The green earth is Your Holy Feet,
The measureless space is the garment You wear;
Mother, I worship Thee with tears of ecstatic devotion.

All faiths sing paeons of Your Supreme Splendour,
You are the sweet essence of Vedas four.
All names, all forms merge into Your Infinite Being.
How can I adore You, Mother, but in awed silence?

Before Creation

[A free rendering of the Nasadiya Suktam, a famous hymn in the Rig Veda (10, 129)]

What could be the cause, the creative impulse
To the primordial life-throb in the all-pervading void?
What could be the Logos, the Divine Seed
Out of which has sprung the universe so vast and varied?

Like sparks from the blazing fire,
Like bubbles from the swelling ocean,
The universe emerges from the Divine Will,
Exists for aeons and dissolves into the primal Cause.

There was neither aught nor naught before creation,
There was neither day nor night;
Only blinding darkness filled everywhere.
Could it be Being or Nothing? Who knows?

There was neither creation nor death;
Who knows for certain what existed then?
But there was the divine spark brooding,
In which was inherent all the potential creation.

Before the great act of creation, so dim and distant,
There was hovering the Spirit, all alone;
It moved on—single—in the limitless expanse, breathing without air,
Becoming the vast many, infilling them with life, yet was One.

It shines of itself, illumining all,
Yet it transcends all, the Supreme One.
All the finite beings, pining for union and shedding the ego,
Merge in It and are fulfilled.

The Jiva sundered from the Supreme, yet longing for merger,
Makes its little life one long act of soulful worship;
Purged, cleansed of all dross of sensuous cravings, all samsaric ties,
It has its final union with the Great Being, the Immortal One.

You are Far, Yet Near

Delay not, my beloved Mother, pouring Your mercy
into my wretched heart;
Orphaned I am in this alien world, alone, helpless,
Give me refuge, my Mother of infinite compassion.

Your are farthest of the far, nearest of the near,
Subtlest of the subtle, greatest of the great,
Pervading everywhere, indwelling all,
The origin of the Pranava Sound begetting worlds
   legion.

You are Perfection, Power, Majesty Supreme,
You are the very essence of all knowledge, all mystery,
You project worlds, sustain, and dissolve them at last,
You revel in creation which is Your endless sport.

Have mercy on me, Mother, awaken my sleeping spirit,
Give me a taste of the nectar of immortality,
Breaker of samsara's bondage, my Divine Mother,
To Thee I cling like a frightened child; forsake me not.

The Holy Confluence

You are the Truth that indwells me,
The infinite Knowledge, Grace and Power incarnate;
But, Your Maya which entices all, makes vain
All my feeble strivings to know 'me'.

'I am in You, You are in me' is the Truth
That gathers You and me into oneness;
My self sundered from You is a fiction,
All that I am is an emanation from Your vast being.

*I come and go, You remain ever,
I seek Your Grace, You give aplenty;
You are the Reality eternal, infinite,
And the varied world is Your wanton Play.

Time ever bows down to Your Holy Feet,
Whence spring up myriad universes,
Which are whirling for aeons, and are moved;
Then who am I, Ma, but Your fancy?

I live and move and have my being in You,
This little 'me' is Your fun.
Mother, give me that intense bliss of eternal union
That I disappear for You to appear alone.*

Will My Krishna Ever Come?

Will Krishna, my Beloved,
ever come, friend?
Will He ever sing with me,
His love-lorn Radha?

Will my Lord ever cheer this poor me pining for Him?
Or has He forgotten all about me, leaving me dying?

Look, do you see afar, my friend,
My blue-complexioned Krishna coming along
   the forest track?
Do you hear the faint distant notes of their rapturous
   melodies
Pouring out from the flute on His hallowed lips?

Ah my dear, I fear my breath may stop,
For the pangs of wrench crush and break my heart.
When my lotus-eyed Krishna comes at last to His sinking
   Radha,
The flickering life of this withered frame will have gone
   out.

Be of cheer, Radha! Can He ever miss You?... Betray
   You?...
Your tears of chastest love are gems in His crown.
But for you, His eternal sweet-heart, His companion age
   after age,
Krishna's flute would have been muted, its melodies
   stilled ere long.

Mother of All

Mother of all, all things and beings,
You are in all, deep within,
As Wisdom Divine, the very nectar of Immortality.

My Mother Amritanandamayi,
You are Love, and Grace, and Wisdom perfect
Destroyer of the seeds of samsara's unending bondage.

You are the dawn of Creation,
The key to the cosmic mystery and deliverance,
Whose Holy Feet even the celestial sages worship.

The Treasure of Experience

I have been sighing and yearning for my Krishna,
Weaving dreams of His eternal abode in my love-sick
    heart;
My eyes have been watching long and are dry,
I have been weeping long and am almost dying.

Yet I know, my Lord, You are the ocean of compassion,
The end and fulfilment of all knowledge, all wisdom,
The final reach of the windy path of all mortals' journey,
The ambient shade cooling and soothing the souls crushed
    and bleeding.

All modes of worship, all prayers and penances go unto You,
You are the infinite nectar flooding hearts soaked in devotion,
The sole refuge of the weary, vexed and lonely caught in samsara's endless whirl,
The All-merciful Lord who lifts and liberates mortals bent low in adoration.

My Heart, A Temple

My fondest Mother, smile Your divine smile,
Pour Your unearthly love into my barren heart,
Dispel all the gloom that grows thick,
Stay ever in me, Mother, never leave.

In my heart's holy shrine
All my musings, meditations ever centre on You;
My little life is one long, soulful adoration
Unto You, my Mother of eternal charm.

My heart is hushed, awed, alert,
I am rapt in prayer, ever expecting Your Grace,
My Beloved Mother, my all, my sole refuge,
Steal in and illumine my sombre soul.

I have been seeking, pining for love,
I am alone, forlorn, dejected;

I have wandered far chasing a vague vision,
and have wept long and am tired.

My parched heart is crushed to pieces,
It is burning, burning in wordless agony.
Won't You lift Your veil at least for once,
Revealing Yourself, Your divine form?

Drive away, Mother, the dark clouds
Weighing on my sinking heart;
Flood it with Your nectarine love, baptise it,
Make it a worthy offering at Your altar.

I do not ask for celestial joys,
Nor for earth's choicest gifts;
All I seek is the all-devouring devotion
Which liberates me for ever from samsara's age-old
    delusion.

Let my tongue ever chant Your holy mantra,
Let my ears ever hear Your Divine voice,
Let my eyes be ever brimful with tears of love,
Let my heart ever revel in the vision of Your Divine
    Form.

Hymn to Ganga

Ah, my Mother Ganga, celestial Ganga,
All-purifying, perennial Bhageerathi,
The Holy Theertha that washes off all sins,
The divine minstrel hurrying down the ages.

You spring from Your eternal home to sanctify the earth;
Countless millions, muttering Your Mantra, plunge in
With the simple faith of a child in its mother,
and emerge thrilled, baptised, transformed.

You rush down from the dizzy heights of
    Mount Himavan,
Ever gurgling, chattering, laughing and singing,
Blithe, blissful like one divinely inspired,
Spreading waves of sheer ecstasy all around.

Ah! My auspicious Ganga, Your very touch transports
    one into trance,
Your frothy waves scatter soul's sweetest melodies;
You are the wealth immortal of Bharat's hoary punya,
You chasten all, exalt all, bless and fulfil all.

Let my Heart Be a Flower at Your Feet

My heart unfolds into a thousand-petaled lotus,
You are seated in its centre as the honey of love, of wisdom.
When my cheeks touch it, all the griefs of my dull yesterdays are no more,
And I am bathed in the bliss of a new life, and am fulfilled.

Like the dulcet music of harmony, Amma delights all,
She exudes the wondrous charm of the all-enfolding soul;
She glides along like a limpid stream with outstretched arms,
Quenching the dire thirst of Her countless children far and near.

In those marvellous eyes wells up Compassion encompassing all,
Flooding the famished earth, renewing and sanctifying it.
Let me have umpteen births, I care not,
My heart will ever be a flower at Her Feet.

May You Fare Well

This is the Holy Land, immortal Bharat,
Sanctified by sages down the ages,
Singing the bliss of Soul in deathless hymns
Away in the past when history was not.

Generations have come and gone down the track of time,
Their spirit has been quickened, enthralled by the
   sonorous hymns of the Vedas.
The heart of Bharat is ever attuned to the lilting music
   of their soul,
It is ever humming soul's rapturous melodies in utter
   Self-forgetfulness.

The Vedas our sages have preserved and left to us,
Unfold the mystery of man, his Truth, his divine Self.
Ages pass, but that vision eternally true is as fresh as the
   dawn.
Time bows to it in awed, silent adoration.

This great land will still ring in exalted joy of the
   Immortal, the Eternal,
The world will still listen and be inspired to larger
   visions, greater goals.
The world in truth is one family, a pretty nest of kindred
   souls,
Fare You well, fare You well, fare You well.

Rain Cloud

My longing heart which is a tiny butterfly,
Sulking in loneliness, tired of long watching,
Is all agog for Your Lotus Face
Wreathed in divine smile, pure and radiant.

My eyes are bedimmed, their light gone,
The yonder light on the sea is dying out.
Like the dew-drop at the far edge of a leaf of grass,
All my hopes are adown, despair darkening my mind.

When will my Mother come home?
My winkless eyes are ever expectant.
When will the note of harmony awake
In my heart now all discordant, clamorous.

Around me is rain raging in torrents,
In me is the scorching heat of separation.
The lone rain-cloud bent with a pitcherful of water
Has sailed off and is seen no more.

Like the fabled bird looking wistfully at the rain-cloud,
How long should I keep watching for Your return, Ma?

My Heart, A Flower at Her Altar

My Mother is the sweet melody of love,
My Mother is the soft rhythm of harmony.
She glides along like a limpid stream
Through countless hearts, cleansing and baptising.

Divinity has incarnated now as the Mother of all,
Pouring in ceaseless Love and Grace
   that lights and liberates,
Illumining the darkened earth, sanctifying it.
Let the little flower of my love-filled heart drop
  at Her Holy Feet.

Peace at Last

My heart folded like a bud in silent salutation
Unfolds into a thousand-petalled lotus of light, delight.
You are enthroned in it as nectarine sweetness, splendour
    divine.
I feel the thrill in every cell, my whole being baptised
    anew.

I kiss the flushed cheeks of the blooming flower of my
    heart,
I taste its honey of tenderest compassion, of love
    boundless;
All the haunting griefs of my dull yesterdays are gone,
My heart now is overflowing with nectar, throwing me
    into raptures.

Dedication

This is the land where the sky was crimsoned
With the radiant rays of the new dawn.
This is the land which offered the finest flowers,
Plucked from the soul, unto the Divine.

This is the land which was stirred and thrilled
By the rapturous melodies poured from the flute of the Lord.
Ah! My Holy Land, blessed with earth's endless bounties,
I dedicate my heart and soul unto Your service in words and deeds.

The long sleep is over, the dark night has ended.
No more shall I sleep, no more shall I slacken.
My beloved land, the haven of my soul,
Hold me fast in my resolve to live and die for You.

The immortal gains of your Tapas, Your sacred wisdom,
The soul-sweetening Bhakti of Your great sons,
Your vision of Mukti liberating one from samsara's
  ceaseless whirl,
The matchless glories of Your music, poesy and arts,
The wondrous saga of Your heroic deeds and valiant
  victories,
May they all inspire my life, making it a worthy offering
  unto You.

Salutation

Your love, so full, pure and chastening
Is ever poured into pious hearts
Which in the silent joy of loving worship
Are lost in Self-forgetfulness.

Many are the blest ones,
Tied to Mother's Feet by chords of love.
You wipe away all their stains, all sins,
Fill them with peace that ever abides.

I see before me the Karthika lamp burning bright,
Illumining the darkened earth with the light divine.
I offer, Holy Mother, my soulful adoration,
Ever awaiting that great dawn of my liberation.

The New Dawn

The new dawn, heralding Divine Glory, will emerge
  anon,
The brooding darkness enveloping the globe will vanish,
The benighted earth will be bathed in the light divine.

Birds will stir up and chirrup, warbling out greeting
   notes,
Flowers galore will bloom, dripping with nectarine honey,
Their luscious smell will be wafted over the earth.
Eyes will open to Truth, light will spread everywhere,
A new joy, a vast peace will descend on one and all.

All the muted sorrows of the human heart will be lifted,
God's refuge that promises new life will beckon all,
The distant memory of the soul's ancient sanctuary will
   wake,
Groping pilgrims, assured of the tryst, will hasten
   straight.

The glorious Day will burst out in a sudden splendour,
Pride and arrogance overblown by the ego will be crushed,
The primordial ignorance blinding the soul will be no
    more.
Fear, doubt and anguish will be stilled,
Wisdom will dawn setting at rest the soul's fearsome
    aches,
Compassion, High Heaven's dearest gift, will flood
All the famished hearts and the barren earth.

Glossary of Sanskrit Terms

Bhakti — Devotion.

Bharat — India.

Dharma — Righteousness, in accordance with Divine Harmony.

Karthika — Mother's birthstar. Lamps are lighted on Karthika days.

Mukti — Liberation from the cycle of birth and death.

Pranava Mantra — The syllable Om.

Punya — Merit. Opposite of sin.

Sadhak — A spiritual aspirant.

Samsara — The world of plurality; the cycle of birth and death.

Sat Chit Ananda — Existence, Consciousness, Bliss, the attributes of Brahman, the Absolute.

Tapas — Literally 'heat'. The practice of spiritual austerities for the sake of self-purification.

"Accept me, Mother, out of Your boundless compassion. Poor me, I have nothing to offer but this frail, unscented flower of my heart; sanctify it with Your touch, make it worthy of being placed at Your feet as my final worship."

Refuge
—Swami Turiyamritananda Puri

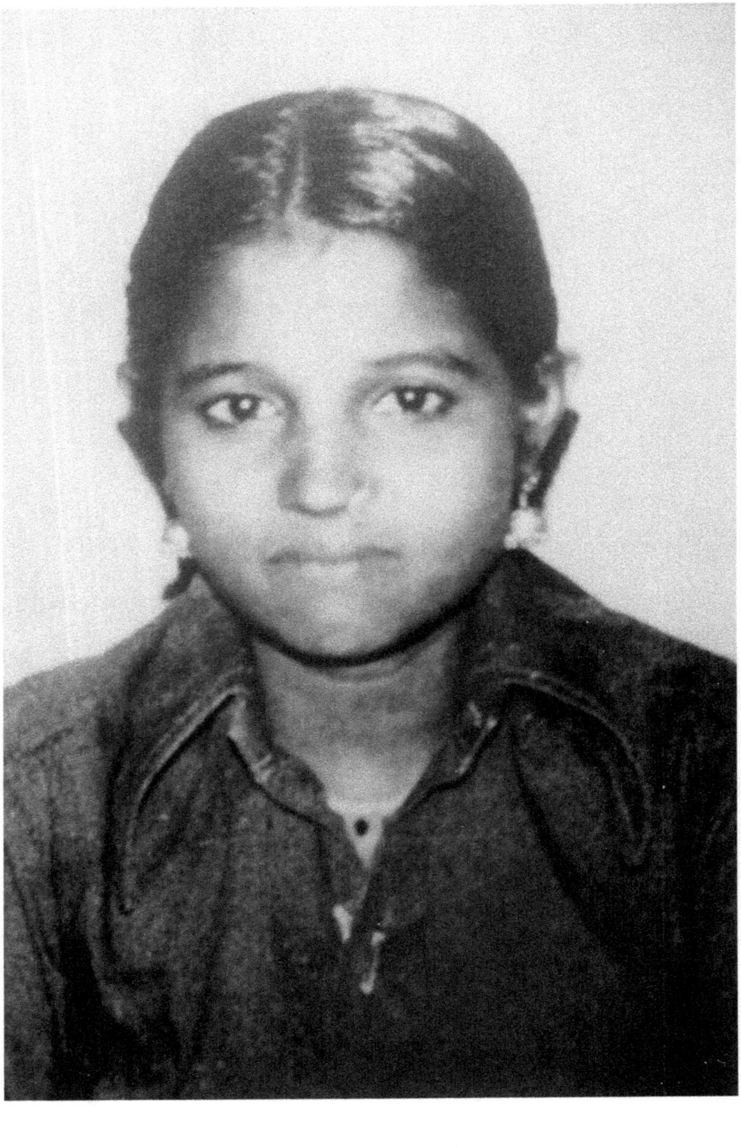

1978, at age 25

www.ingramcontent.com/pod-product-compliance
Lightning Source LLC
Chambersburg PA
CBHW060340050426
42449CB00011B/2805